# ERRATA

The last two lines of the pages below, from the song "Sooner or Later," should have the corr
stated here.

Page 20

Page 44

Page 62

Page 86

**HAL•LEONARD**

**JAZZ PLAY-ALONG**

Book and CD for B♭, E♭, C and Bass Clef Instruments

# SONDHEIM

**volume 183**

Arranged and Produced
by Mark Taylor

BOOK

CD

| TITLE | PAGE NUMBERS | | | |
| --- | --- | --- | --- | --- |
| | C Treble Instruments | B♭ Instruments | E♭ Instruments | C Bass Instruments |
| Another Hundred People | 22 | 25 | 64 | 67 |
| Being Alive | 4 | 28 | 46 | 70 |
| Good Thing Going | 6 | 30 | 48 | 72 |
| The Ladies Who Lunch | 8 | 32 | 50 | 74 |
| Losing My Mind | 10 | 34 | 52 | 76 |
| No One Is Alone | 12 | 36 | 54 | 78 |
| Not While I'm Around | 14 | 38 | 56 | 80 |
| Pretty Women | 16 | 40 | 58 | 82 |
| Send in the Clowns | 18 | 42 | 60 | 84 |
| Sooner or Later (I Always Get My Man) | 20 | 44 | 62 | 86 |

| TITLE | CD Track Number Split Track/Melody | CD Track Number Full Stereo Track |
| --- | --- | --- |
| Another Hundred People | 1 | 2 |
| Being Alive | 3 | 4 |
| Good Thing Going | 5 | 6 |
| The Ladies Who Lunch | 7 | 8 |
| Losing My Mind | 9 | 10 |
| No One Is Alone | 11 | 12 |
| Not While I'm Around | 13 | 14 |
| Pretty Women | 15 | 16 |
| Send in the Clowns | 17 | 18 |
| Sooner or Later (I Always Get My Man) | 19 | 20 |
| B♭ Tuning Notes | | 21 |

ISBN 978-1-4803-8549-8

## RILTING MUSIC, INC.

EXCLUSIVELY DISTRIBUTED BY

**HAL•LEONARD®**
CORPORATION
7777 W. BLUEMOUND RD. P.O. BOX 13819 MILWAUKEE, WI 53213

Visit Hal Leonard Online at
**www.halleonard.com**

# SONDHEIM

## Volume 183

## Arranged and Produced
## by Mark Taylor

### Featured Players:

**Graham Breedlove–Trumpet/Flugelhorn**
**John Desalme–Saxes**
**Tony Nalker–Keyboards**
**Jim Roberts–Guitar**
**Paul Henry–Bass**
**Todd Harrison–Drums**

## Recorded at Bias Studios, Springfield, Virginia
## Bob Dawson, Engineer

## HOW TO USE THE CD:

Each song has <u>two</u> tracks:

### 1) Split Track/Melody

**Woodwind, Brass, Keyboard,** and **Mallet Players** can use this track as a learning tool for melody style and inflection.

**Bass Players** can learn and perform with this track – remove the recorded bass track by turning down the volume on the LEFT channel.

**Keyboard** and **Guitar Players** can learn and perform with this track – remove the recorded piano part by turning down the volume on the RIGHT channel.

### 2) Full Stereo Track

**Soloists** or **Groups** can learn and perform with this accompaniment track with the RHYTHM SECTION only.

# BEING ALIVE
## FROM COMPANY

MUSIC AND LYRICS BY
STEPHEN SONDHEIM

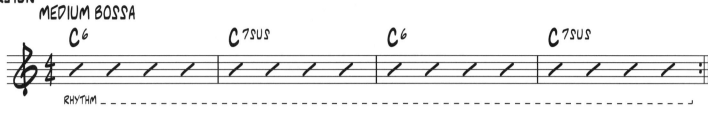

# GOOD THING GOING
### FROM MERRILY WE ROLL ALONG

WORDS AND MUSIC BY
STEPHEN SONDHEIM

# THE LADIES WHO LUNCH

FROM COMPANY

MUSIC AND LYRICS BY
STEPHEN SONDHEIM

# LOSING MY MIND
### FROM FOLLIES

MUSIC AND LYRICS BY
STEPHEN SONDHEIM

# NO ONE IS ALONE

FROM INTO THE WOODS

WORDS AND MUSIC BY
STEPHEN SONDHEIM

CD
11 : SPLIT TRACK/MELODY
12 : FULL STEREO TRACK

C VERSION

# NOT WHILE I'M AROUND

FROM SWEENEY TODD

WORDS AND MUSIC BY
STEPHEN SONDHEIM

C VERSION

# PRETTY WOMEN
## FROM SWEENEY TODD

WORDS AND MUSIC BY
STEPHEN SONDHEIM

CD
17 : SPLIT TRACK/MELODY
18 : FULL STEREO TRACK

C VERSION

# SEND IN THE CLOWNS

FROM THE MUSICAL A LITTLE NIGHT MUSIC

WORDS AND MUSIC BY
STEPHEN SONDHEIM

# Sooner or Later
## (I Always Get My Man)
### FROM THE FILM DICK TRACY

WORDS AND MUSIC BY
STEPHEN SONHEIM

# ANOTHER HUNDRED PEOPLE

FROM COMPANY

MUSIC AND LYRICS BY
STEPHEN SONDHEIM

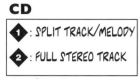

C VERSION

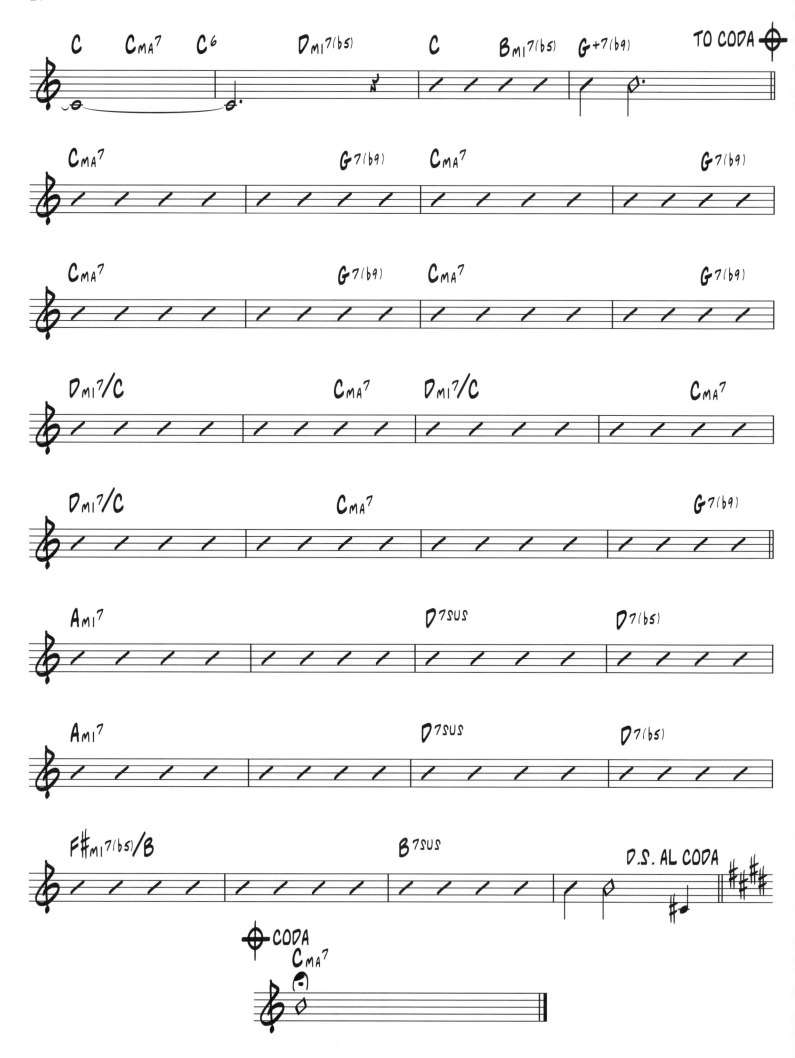

# ANOTHER HUNDRED PEOPLE
### FROM COMPANY

MUSIC AND LYRICS BY
STEPHEN SONDHEIM

**1** : SPLIT TRACK/MELODY
**2** : FULL STEREO TRACK

**Bb VERSION**

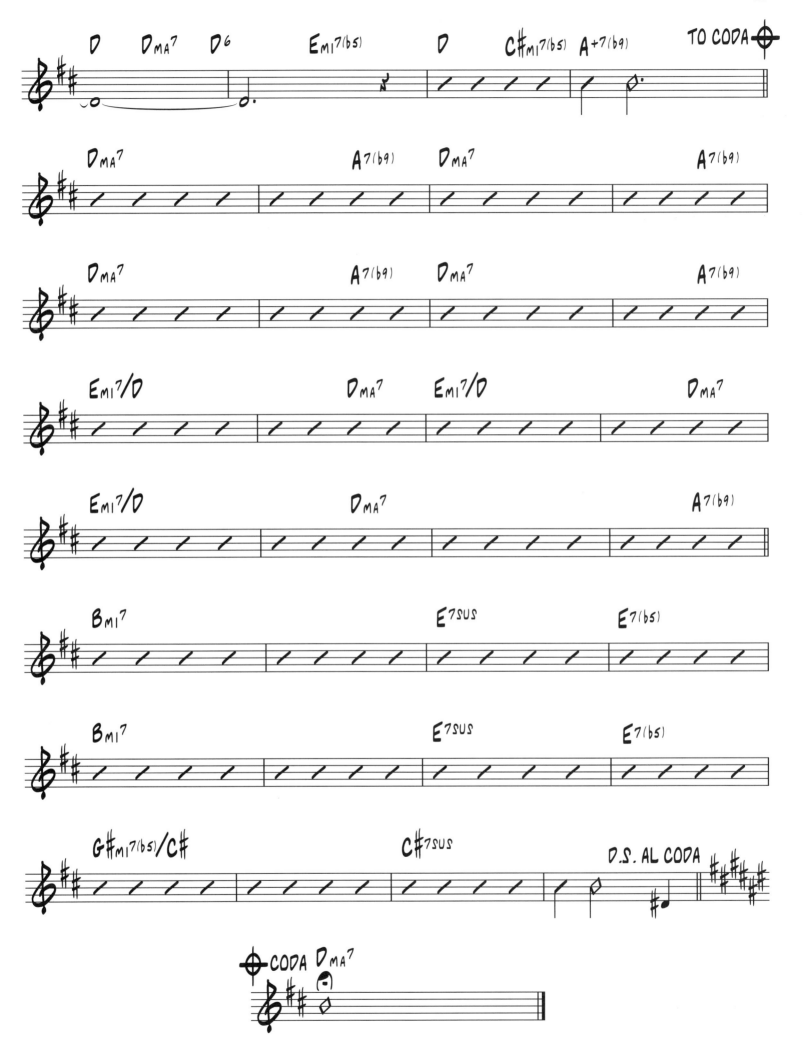

# BEING ALIVE
### FROM COMPANY

MUSIC AND LYRICS BY
STEPHEN SONDHEIM

Bb VERSION

# THE LADIES WHO LUNCH
### FROM COMPANY

MUSIC AND LYRICS BY
STEPHEN SONDHEIM

Bb VERSION

MEDIUM BOSSA

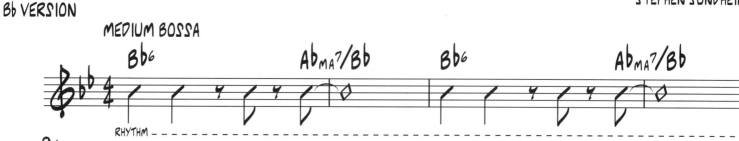

# LOSING MY MIND

FROM FOLLIES

MUSIC AND LYRICS BY
STEPHEN SONDHEIM

Bb VERSION

# NO ONE IS ALONE

### FROM INTO THE WOODS

WORDS AND MUSIC BY
STEPHEN SONDHEIM

**Bb VERSION**

# NOT WHILE I'M AROUND

FROM SWEENEY TODD

WORDS AND MUSIC BY
STEPHEN SONDHEIM

Bb VERSION

# PRETTY WOMEN

**FROM SWEENEY TODD**

WORDS AND MUSIC BY
STEPHEN SONDHEIM

# SEND IN THE CLOWNS
## FROM THE MUSICAL A LITTLE NIGHT MUSIC

WORDS AND MUSIC BY
STEPHEN SONDHEIM

CD
17: SPLIT TRACK/MELODY
18: FULL STEREO TRACK

Bb VERSION

# Sooner or Later
## (I Always Get My Man)
### FROM THE FILM DICK TRACY

Bb VERSION

WORDS AND MUSIC BY
STEPHEN SONHEIM

# BEING ALIVE
## FROM COMPANY

MUSIC AND LYRICS BY
STEPHEN SONDHEIM

Eb VERSION

# GOOD THING GOING
## FROM MERRILY WE ROLL ALONG

WORDS AND MUSIC BY
STEPHEN SONDHEIM

Eb VERSION

# THE LADIES WHO LUNCH
FROM COMPANY

MUSIC AND LYRICS BY
STEPHEN SONDHEIM

Eb VERSION

# Losing My Mind
## FROM FOLLIES

MUSIC AND LYRICS BY
STEPHEN SONDHEIM

**CD**
- ◆9 : SPLIT TRACK/MELODY
- ◆10 : FULL STEREO TRACK

E♭ VERSION

MEDIUM JAZZ BALLAD

# NO ONE IS ALONE
FROM INTO THE WOODS

WORDS AND MUSIC BY
STEPHEN SONDHEIM

Eb VERSION

# NOT WHILE I'M AROUND

FROM SWEENEY TODD

WORDS AND MUSIC BY
STEPHEN SONDHEIM

Eb VERSION

# PRETTY WOMEN

FROM SWEENEY TODD

WORDS AND MUSIC BY
STEPHEN SONDHEIM

# Send in the Clowns
FROM THE MUSICAL A LITTLE NIGHT MUSIC

WORDS AND MUSIC BY
STEPHEN SONDHEIM

CD
19 : SPLIT TRACK/MELODY
20 : FULL STEREO TRACK

# SOONER OR LATER
## (I ALWAYS GET MY MAN)
### FROM THE FILM DICK TRACY

Eb VERSION

WORDS AND MUSIC BY
STEPHEN SONHEIM

# ANOTHER HUNDRED PEOPLE

### FROM COMPANY

MUSIC AND LYRICS BY
STEPHEN SONDHEIM

CD
1: SPLIT TRACK/MELODY
2: FULL STEREO TRACK

Eb VERSION

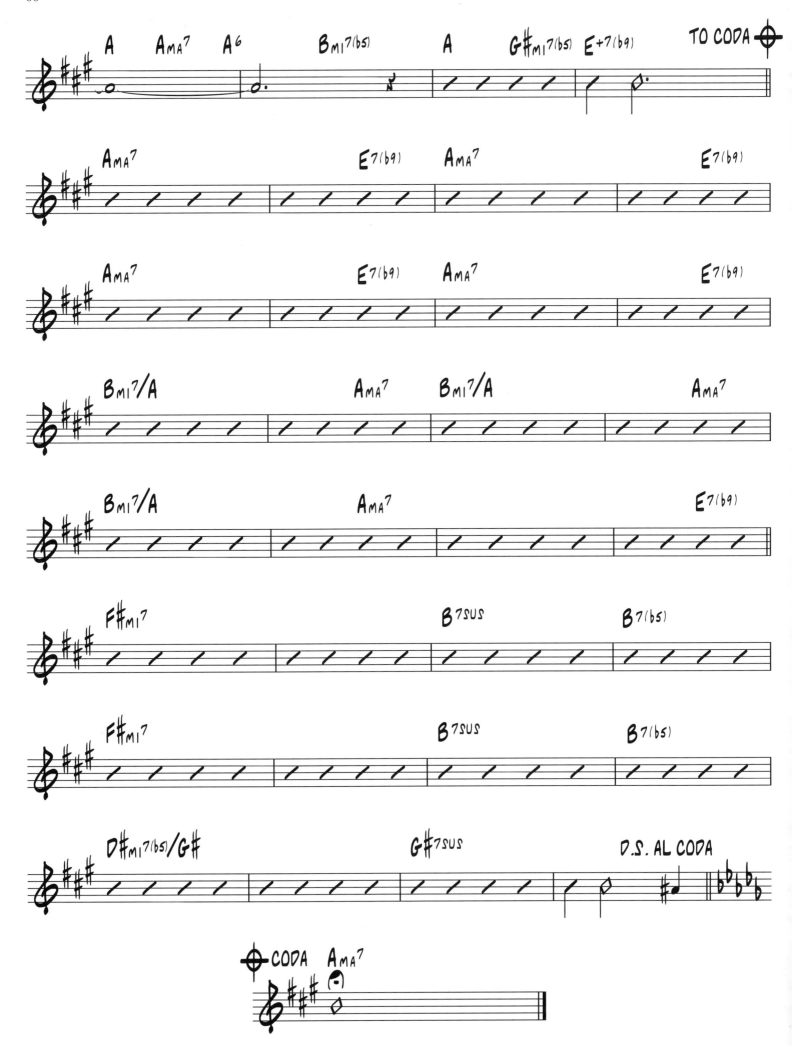

# ANOTHER HUNDRED PEOPLE

FROM COMPANY

MUSIC AND LYRICS BY
STEPHEN SONDHEIM

𝄢: C VERSION

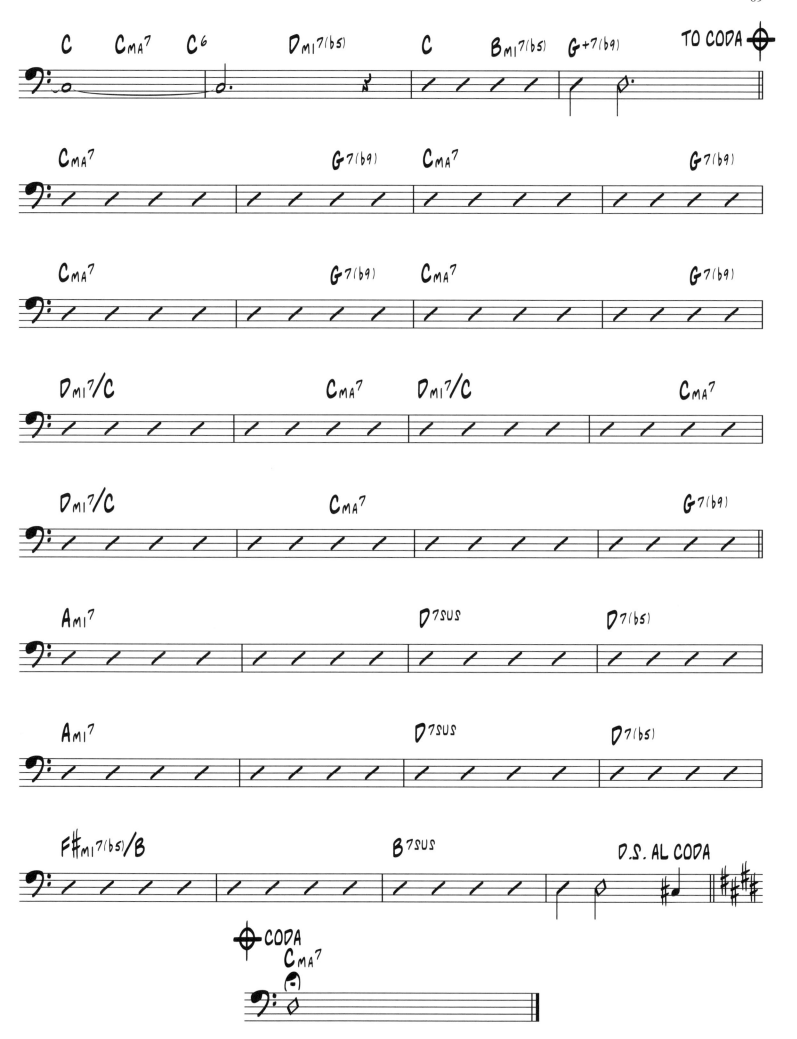

# BEING ALIVE
### FROM COMPANY

MUSIC AND LYRICS BY
STEPHEN SONDHEIM

# GOOD THING GOING

FROM MERRILY WE ROLL ALONG

WORDS AND MUSIC BY
STEPHEN SONDHEIM

# THE LADIES WHO LUNCH
### FROM COMPANY

MUSIC AND LYRICS BY
STEPHEN SONDHEIM

**CD**
◆ 9 : SPLIT TRACK/MELODY
◆ 10 : FULL STEREO TRACK

# LOSING MY MIND
*FROM FOLLIES*

MUSIC AND LYRICS BY
STEPHEN SONDHEIM

𝄢: C VERSION

MEDIUM JAZZ BALLAD

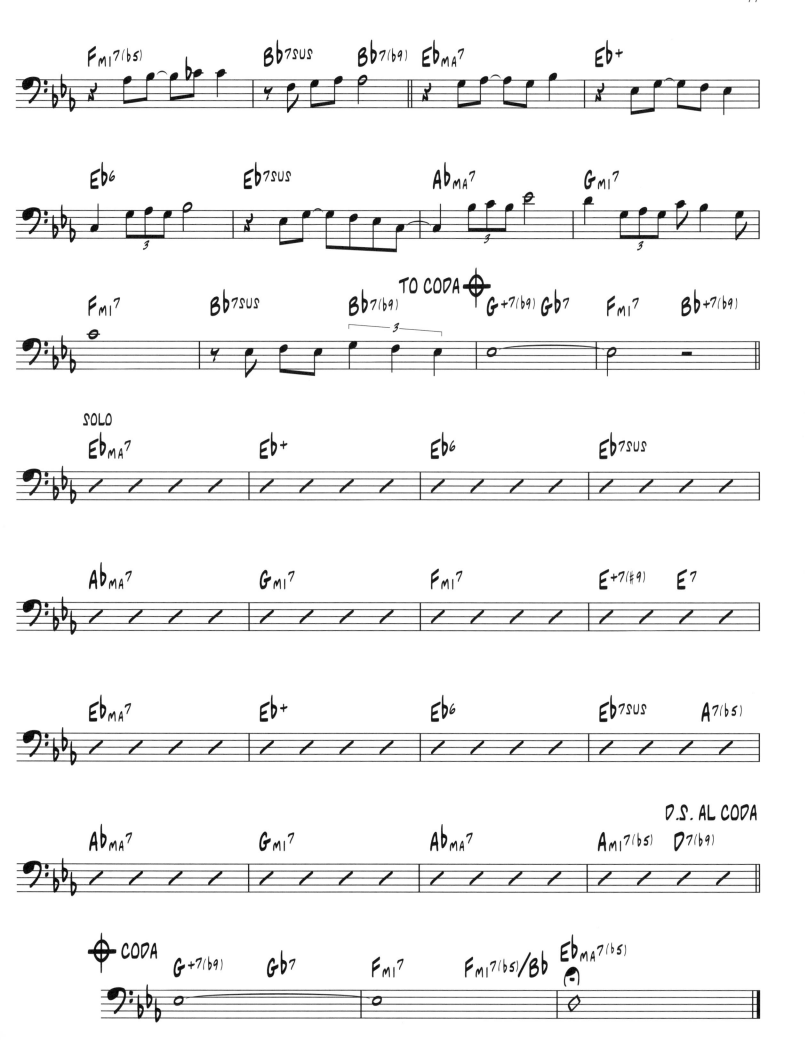

# NO ONE IS ALONE

FROM INTO THE WOODS

WORDS AND MUSIC BY
STEPHEN SONDHEIM

𝄢: C VERSION

# NOT WHILE I'M AROUND
FROM SWEENEY TODD

WORDS AND MUSIC BY
STEPHEN SONDHEIM

# PRETTY WOMEN
FROM SWEENEY TODD

WORDS AND MUSIC BY
STEPHEN SONDHEIM

RIT.

SEND IN THE CLOWNS

FROM THE MUSICAL A LITTLE NIGHT MUSIC

WORDS AND MUSIC BY
STEPHEN SONDHEIM

# SOONER OR LATER
## (I ALWAYS GET MY MAN)
### FROM THE FILM DICK TRACY

WORDS AND MUSIC BY
STEPHEN SONHEIM